A JILLION WAYS

TO SAY GOODBYE TO YOUR PET

Written by Sandra Spring

Illustrated by Max Alnutt

A Jillion Ways Publishing
Helping adults talk to kids about the difficult things in life.

A Jillion Feelings — All Mixed Together
When a pet you love dies,
There are a jillion ways to say goodbye.

Memories Together
Our feelings change and don't last forever,
But memories and love always keep us together.

Forever Friends
A pet is part of your family and always your friend,
And death doesn't mean that has to end.

Why?
Your feelings are important and you will question why,
The things we love in life have to die.

Everything Ends
In this world all living things have an end,
So time is special with family, pets, and friends.

Feelings Aren't Strange
Your pet loved you and that won't change,
Your many, many, many feelings are normal — not strange.

Full of Feelings
This book is full of many feelings that you can try,
When missing your pet there are a jillion ways to say goodbye.

Crying...
Crying makes our faces all wet,
But crying is a great way to say goodbye to your pet.

So cry your tears until you run out of breath,
Because your pet is always with you, even in death.

Smiling...
It's okay to smile when a pet goes away,
Memories of play and laughter are always here to stay.

Pets are funny and give us the giggles,
So laugh out loud until your body wiggles.

Quiet...
Don't say a word or make a sound,
Sometimes not talking helps memories stick around.

Silence doesn't mean you have nothing to say,
Being quiet shows how you feel, and that's okay.

Angry...
Get mad, get loud, and be angry for a while,
Say goodbye to your pet in your own style.

Stomp your feet and let it all out,
Losing something you love can make you want to shout!

Sad...
Put your hands on your face and sit all alone,
Being sad means you wish your pet was at home.

**Other people can't always make you happy when you're sad,
But sadness isn't forever, and that's not so bad.**

Happy...
Jump for joy and remember all the fun,
You loved your pet and having a special loved one.

Clap your hands and think of all the play,
Be happy you had a special pet day after day.

Helpless...
Sometimes we wish we could save our pet,
And when they are hurt, sick, or old we take them to the vet.

But wishes are not enough to save lives,
And it's not your fault if your pet dies.

Guilty...
Sometimes accidents are why pets die,
But accidents are mistakes, and not who we are inside.

Life is difficult when people make mistakes,
But pets love us always, no matter what it takes.

Lonely...
Your feelings of loneliness belong only to you,
Sometimes you need to be alone to know what to do.

So go somewhere special and think for yourself,
Saying goodbye can be lonely — and for no one else.

A Jillion Ways...
There are a jillion ways to say goodbye,
From smiling ear-to-ear to wanting to cry.

A mix of many feelings is what all people do,
Because losing a pet is what other people know too.

Point to the feelings you are feeling now...

Draw a picture of your pet...

Draw a picture of your feelings...

Draw a picture of who you talk to about your feelings...

Write a story about your pet...

Pet Memory Celebration

Ask family and friends to share their feelings and write them down...

Name:

_____

_____

_____

_____

_____

_____

_____

_____

_____

Feeling:

_____

_____

_____

_____

_____

_____

_____

_____

_____

Made in the USA
Las Vegas, NV
07 July 2023

74342346R00024